Nelson Sullivan

The Portapak Prince

by Gary LeGault

Starwalk Press

on the cover:

Nelson Sullivan in Chelsea

(colored pencil drawing by Gary LeGault)

published by

Starwalk Press

U.S.A.

Table of Contents

Prologue

This book contains my impressions of Nelson Sullivan as I recall them. Many others knew Mr. Sullivan and have their own stories to tell. But to me, he was a friend and neighbor before his career as a videographer began. In recounting our adventures together, I hope not to have left anyone out, nor to have misrepresented the facts of our relationship. He was a rare and distinguished fellow in the bustling world of New York during the 1980's, where art openings would happen almost every night in the various fields of entertainment. Nelson was always eager to accept invitations to these gala events, although I sometimes chose to decline them. Perhaps if he had stayed at home occasionally to rest, he would be alive today to write an autobiography. But we have his video tapes, over nineteen-hundred hours of recorded information. This means that he would have been out incrementally taking pictures hundreds of times every year from the day when he first acquired a video camera until his death in 1989.

He was, indeed, a very busy boy.

1. Detail from Nelson in Chelsea (1984)

Chapter 1

In the spring of 1982, I had been living in New York for almost eleven years when *Ina and Bruno*, a movie I'd completed during the late 1970's, appeared on Manhattan Cable Television's Public Access Channel D. In those days, cable television was a relatively new medium, and all one needed to do was to call the station and book sufficient time to exhibit an original work. There was little or no competition, because most people did not have access to video cameras, nor the editing equipment to put together a feature-length program. To publicize my movie, I ran around Manhattan, slapping up posters with a bucket of wallpaper paste and a brush. After staying up all night to accomplish this task, I remember pasting a poster onto the wall of a brick building just off Fifth Avenue near 73rd Street when I noticed a young Robert Dinero dressed in a wool coat, staring at me while I labored. The poster was colorful and eye-catching. I'd learned this technique from my junior high school friend, Tracy Tubb's father (a commercial artist), who had created lovely silk-screened prints for his daughter when she ran for student body treasurer at our middle school, many years earlier in California. It always pays to be observant, especially when an artwork is painstakingly done, for there is much to be gleaned from the achievements of others.

My posters were visible all over New York. At the time, I was working in the Butterick Building as a file room manager for the architectural firm of *Howard, Needles, Tammen and Bergendoff*, where even some of the draftsmen had seen this advertisement and were surprised to recognize my name as the film's creator. I'll never know how many people actually watched my rambling melodrama, a madcap romp through the imaginative world of a Hollywood hairdresser and an eastern roller derby queen, because I received little or no response from anyone about it, until one day

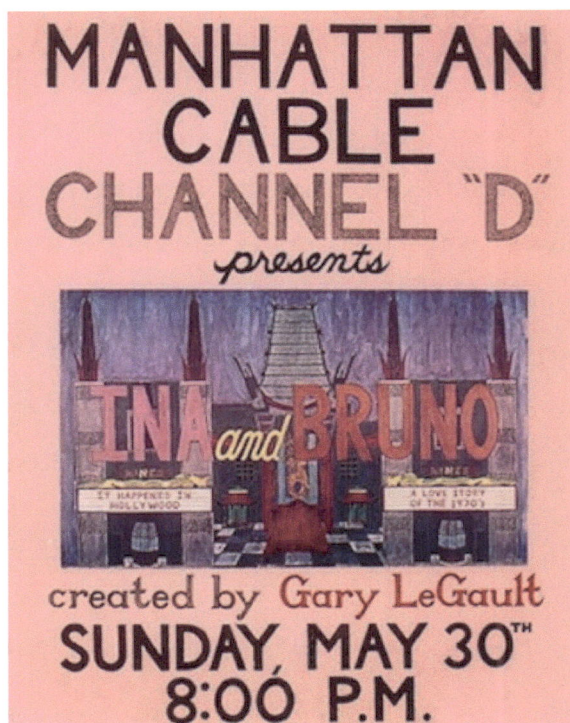

2. Ina and Bruno poster (1982)

a letter arrived from a certain Mister Gary Kanter, telling me how much he enjoyed my vision that had come to life on his television set that Sunday evening in May of 1982.

Apparently, he'd found my address in the Manhattan telephone directory, and sent me my first (and only) piece of fan mail. I was alarmed by this, fearing that he was overly enthused and that I should proceed with caution. Finally, I agreed to meet him at Joe Allen's Restaurant in the theater district, and brought along my trusted neighbor and behind-the-scenes assistant, Morgan Moffatt, just to ensure my safety in the presence of a stranger.

Gary Kanter was as sweet as he could be, however, and about as menacing as a funny valentine when I presented him with a press kit from the movie, thinking that it would appease him and he'd go away satisfied. But Gary persisted, asking for permission to call me up sometime and get together again. "I *loved* your movie," he said. "Here you are, living in New York and creating so much beauty, you really ought to meet other people who are of the same mind. Why don't I introduce you to Nelson Sullivan? He's been talking about getting a video camera for ages. I think he would enjoy meeting you. Let me call him up."

Unfortunately, Nelson had not watched the screening of *Ina and Bruno* on Manhattan Cable Television, but had seen the poster and wondered what the film was about, before Gary Kanter called to tell him that we had met. Conveniently, Nelson lived down Ninth Avenue about seven blocks from my apartment in Chelsea. So, when Nelson telephoned one day, I dropped by his three-story townhouse to become acquainted.

Nelson was all charm and pleasant manners, exhibiting the grace that had been bestowed upon him as a southern gentleman growing up in the small town of Kershaw, South Carolina. "I've been thinking about getting a video camera for years," he said. "Do you have a copy of your movie on VHS?" When I responded that indeed, I had, he asked, "Why don't you bring it over one afternoon, and we'll watch your film together?" And that's how our friendship began.

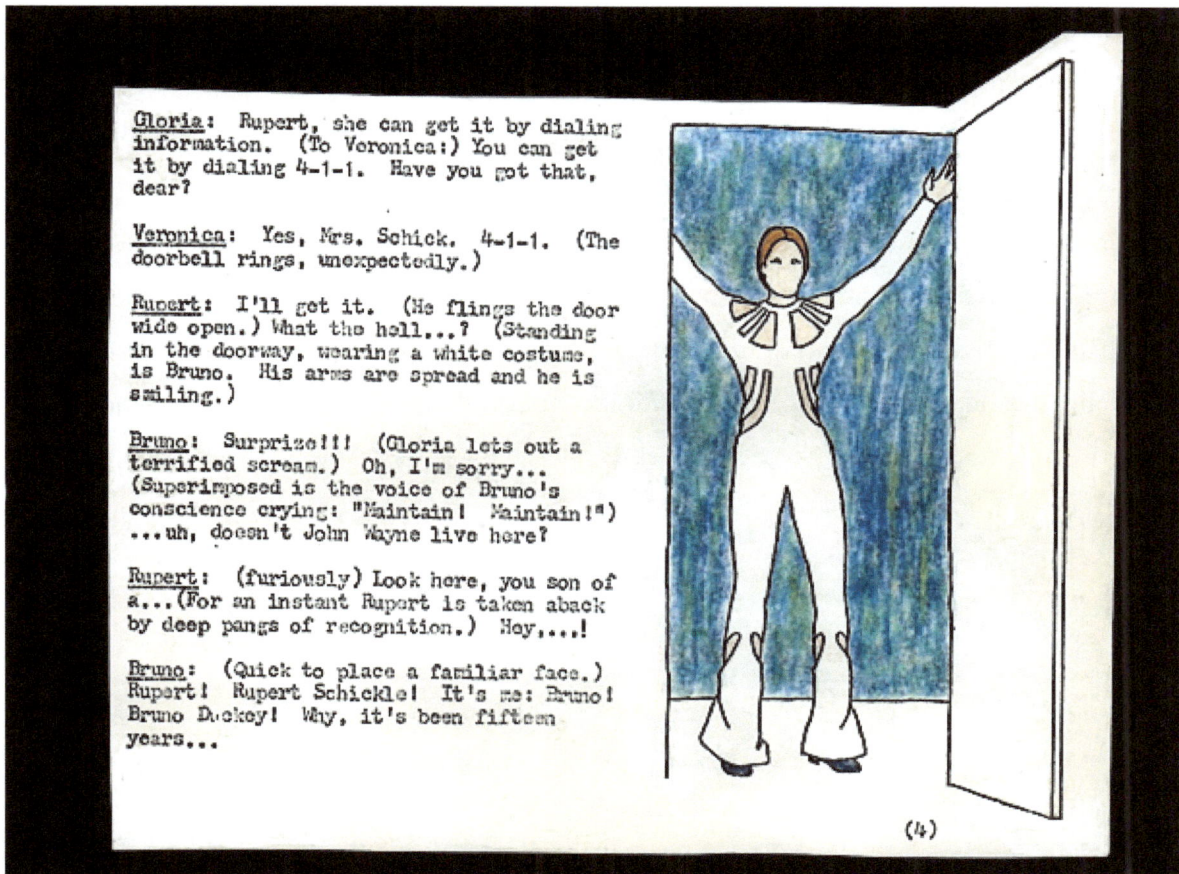

3. *Detail from the illustrated manuscript of Ina and Bruno*

Ina and Bruno had been written in the basement of a tenement building where I lived in Chelsea during the winter of 1971-72. It was an ambitious project, set on the west coast, despite the fact that most of it was performed before painted, cardboard backdrops at my three-room flat in New York. I am embarrassed by the film today, although at the time it seemed like a worthy endeavor. The dialog was peppered with profanity and unsavory allusions, the characters were archetypical, and the cast included almost every out of work actor in New York. But Nelson didn't seem to mind, and laughed in all of the appropriate places, as we watched this fractured tale unfold onto his television screen one Sunday afternoon. "That was wonderful," he said. "Thank you for sharing it with me. I've been thinking of buying a video camera for a long time, and taking it with me around New York to document all of the exciting things that are happening here."

He decided immediately that we should become friends and made every effort to include me in his schedule. He had a relaxed way of approaching things, whereas I was openly ambitious and unwilling to be deterred by any obstacle that stood in the way of my desire to succeed in the visual arts. Indeed, I was quite full of myself, for life had not yet knocked the stuffing out of me (as eventually, it would). I tried not to exhibit outward signs of conceit, but to be a bit in awe of my ability, resourcefulness and occasional good fortune.

Nelson, in contrast, had grace and humility and a southern accent that was completely disarming. He also had honorable intentions in everything he did. He was like a sweet, adorable child, puffing on cigarettes and dashing around in linen suits, pretending to be completely grown up, yet delighting in each new experience with the enchantment of a precocious teenager.

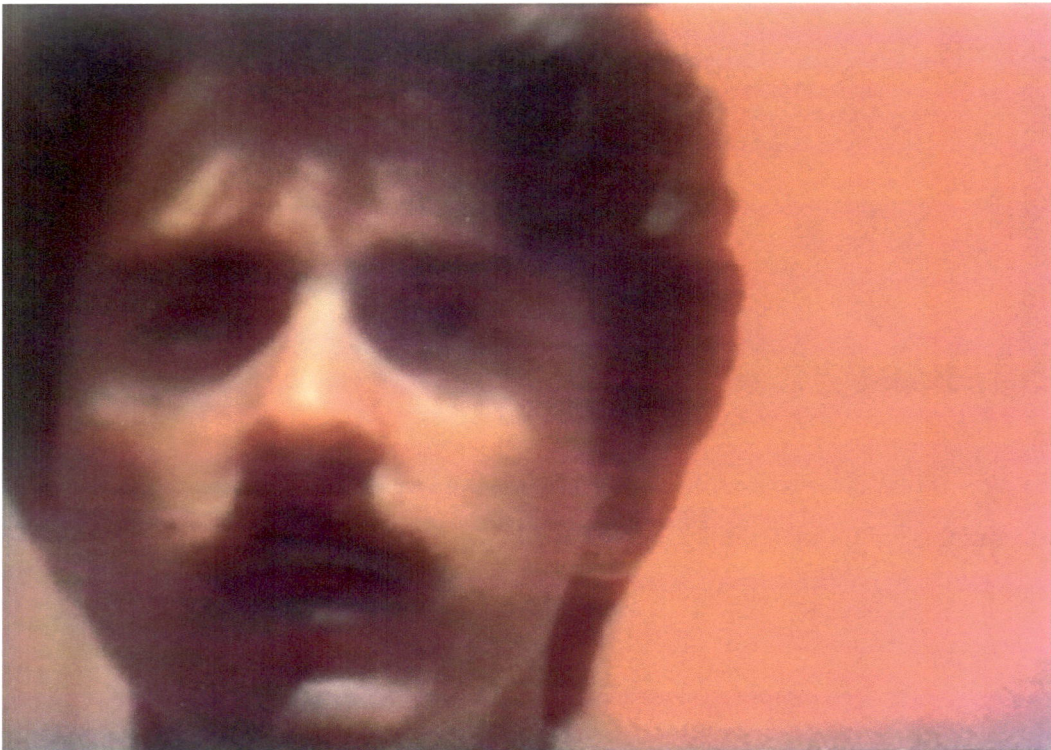

4. A youthful Nelson (1983)

He would often telephone me in the evening, after I had returned from work, and invite me to his house, where he would regale me with stories of his youth in South Carolina, and sometimes we would go out from there for walks along the Hudson River with his affectionate dog, Blackout, who obtained his name during the great power outage of 1977.

There was a full-sized apartment on the ground floor of his building in which he housed his partner, a Japanese businessman, named Choux (whose full name now escapes me). Choux was very quiet, but protective of Nelson, and at our first introduction we locked glances, as if there were some sort of contest between us, but as time went by the tension gradually began to subside.

When the parlor game, *Trivial Pursuit*, came out we spent several evenings seated around the table in Nelson's kitchen with my friend, Morgan Moffatt, and Nelson's roommate, Choux, who struggled to answer questions regarding topics that were familiar for those brought up in western culture, yet challenging to a man of Japanese descent. Choux, who was a model of politeness, did amazingly well, however, and we were always surprised by his thoughtful answers, even though he sometimes had difficulty in pronouncing the English words.

Nelson had interesting friends and loved hosting them at parties in his living room. Among them were Michael Musto, Albert Crudo, Sylvia Miles, Rhonda Granger and her boyfriend, Brant Mewborn. Rhonda was a beautiful blonde from the midwest, who resembled a modern version of Jean Harlow or Marilyn Monroe. She was very sweet by nature, as was the young Michael Musto and his friend, Albert Crudo, who used to show up for Nelson's parties with the most impish gleam in his eye, often giggling with Michael about some private joke that was going on between them. Choux would watch patiently from the background until these parties were in full swing, then quietly disappear down the stairs to his quarters below, resurfacing to browse the contents of Nelson's refrigerator as the evening wore on. There was a cat, a dog, a roommate, familiar friends and a lovely ebb and flow to Nelson's life in the first few years of our friendship. He had an upright Steinway piano at one end of his living room near the street-facing windows, and once in a while he would play for us, tapping very lightly on the keys.

During the day, Nelson worked part-time at Patelson's Music Store near Carnegie Hall, where classical musicians could find the precise pieces of sheet music that they required for their particular instruments. Nelson had attended music school as a child, and seemed well-suited to his job. Sometimes, he would invite Morgan and me to meet him after work, and we would watch him running around the store, pulling pieces of sheet music out of carefully catalogued drawers for each customer, before leaving for the day with his eagerly awaiting friends. Even though his family in South Carolina provided him with a monthly stipend, he supplemented his income by working for Mr. Patelson on weekdays between 10:00 a.m. and 2:00 o'clock in the afternoon. Afterward, he would be at liberty to explore the sights and sounds of New York, where there was always something interesting for him to enjoy.

Gary Kanter, who had introduced us, did not frequent Nelson's parties, but occasionally would appear with his significant other, Eugene Neely, more often stopping to visit me by himself at my apartment on West 21st Street, where things would usually be happening on a much smaller scale.

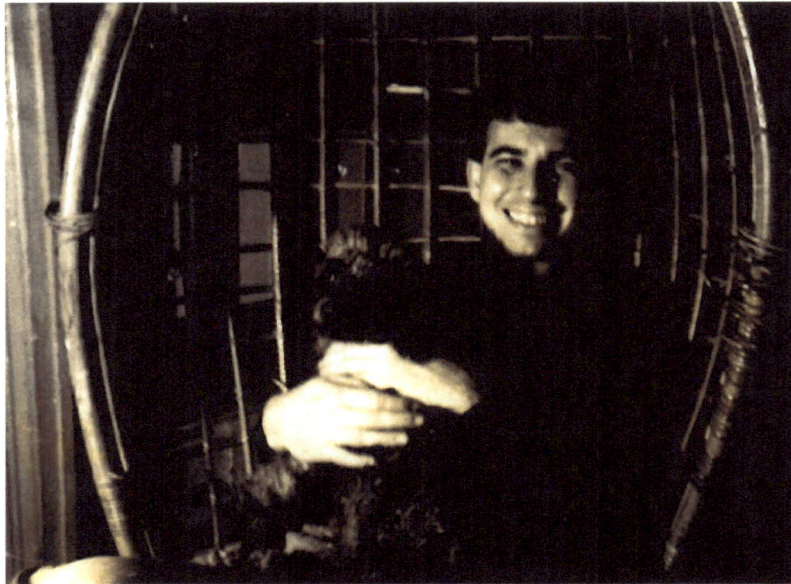

5. *Gary Kanter with the author's dog, Mandy (1983)*

Gary Kanter held a job at the W. & J. Sloane furniture store in New York, and lived in the West Thirties, not far from Macy's and Gimble's department stores. Originally from Kansas City, Missouri, he had come to New York years earlier with Eugene and thoroughly enjoyed living in Manhattan. As the years went by, I would learn that he was also extremely talented, not only as an interior designer, but as a portrait artist, with a unique style of drawing and a vivid sense of color.

At one point, Gary decided to try his skill at acting and telephoned to say that he was in a new play, somewhere in Greenwich Village (the theater's location eludes me at this time), and invited me to come and watch a performance. Nelson was happy to tag along, and we enjoyed seeing Gary perform among the other young actors, until suddenly there was a pause on stage during which an embarrassing moment occurred. Nelson and I were sitting in the front row intently gazing at the scene (which would have been enough to make anyone feel nervous), but refrained from laughing over the apparent mishap. Sometimes things go terribly wrong on stage, but Gary recovered by casting a sidelong glance and speaking his next line as though nothing out of the ordinary had happened. It was a quick recovery, and he skillfully prevented this play of manners from becoming a "whodunnit."

On the way home, however, we stopped at a telephone booth near White Tower Hamburgers on Eighth Avenue at 14th Street, where I accidentally squeezed Nelson's thumb into the closing metal door. This turned out to be a painful mistake and poor Nelson's thumbnail eventually fell off, but grew back several weeks later (thankfully). He was a good sport about it, despite the anguish of spending an evening gadding about town with someone as reckless as me.

Nelson didn't drink alcohol. As he once explained, he had been a drinker for many years, but finally stopped, because odd things had begun to happen as a result of his drinking. He'd operated a beauty shop on Fire Island during the early 1970's when New York society was rampantly running wild. There were times when he'd wake up following a previous night's escapade, and find himself surrounded by several unexpected consequences. Even so, he was smart enough to have realized the error of his ways and only on sacred holidays thereafter, would he allow himself to have an occasional glass of wine.

He had a passion for collecting footwear. This was long before Imelda Marcos and her similar penchant came to the public's attention, but Nelson's third floor bedroom was filled with many pairs of unusual and variously styled shoes. He appeared to be a bit of a dandy when he would step out wearing a dapper sportscoat, a clever necktie and a snazzy pair of shoes.

During the first year of our friendship, Nelson would visit my apartment in Chelsea occasionally, and join the guests there in a game of Scrabble. William F. Miller had lost his apartment in the East Village, and moved in with me for a while. Bill was an avid Scrabble player and often would get into disputes with Nelson over the spelling or authenticity of a particular word. Their quarrels would ultimately be resolved by consulting Webster's American Dictionary. These were very orderly gatherings, and at one of our parlor game nights, Nelson was introduced to the actor and man about town, James W. Gallagher. Jamie had just come from his performance in the play, *I Died Yesterday*, starring Jackie Curtis in the role of the motion picture actress, Frances Farmer. There was an ironic connection between an event in Frances Farmer's life and a major occurrence in Nelson's own family. But none of this was discussed at Jamie's first meeting with Nelson at my apartment in Chelsea. This was shortly before Nelson had acquired his first video camera, and at that time, *I* would video tape *Nelson* with my SONY

AV 8400 recorder and camera, a heavy reel-to-reel contraption that I had purchased, prior to the advent of more compact, consumer cameras that were to follow.

6. *Nelson Sullivan, Elmer Kline and Bill Miller in a game of Scrabble*

I had purchased my first video camera in 1977 as a way of preserving my own theatrical productions. Presenting an original play on off-off Broadway was always a short-lived ordeal, and once the play's run was over, each performance seemed to be forever lost to those who were not in attendance. By acquiring a video camera, I thought that I had solved this problem, but more often than not, I would be enticed to videotape the work of other performers. Jackie Curtis was particularly skilled at persuading me to videotape his appearances, as was Sister Tui. I resisted, at first, but these two actors were so determined, that eventually I caved in. It had never been my purpose to document the work of other artists. I bought the camera for my own personal use. But in hindsight, it's fortunate that I yielded to the requests of others, or I wouldn't have photographed some of the subjects who loomed very large in my early life. It was a simple matter of being in the right place at the right time. I also liked the instant quality of video tape.

Once a motion picture had been shot on video tape, it could immediately be reviewed. For this reason, I also liked taking Polaroid photographs.

One day, Nelson called me up to tell me that he'd purchased his first video camera. He asked me to stop by his house and watch him take the camera out of its box. I arrived with my dear friend and neighbor, Morgan Moffatt, and we joined a small party in the kitchen. Nelson was very excited about being able to record anything that came into view and turned the camera toward us. "But, Nelson," I asked, "Why are you filming? There's nothing interesting going on." But Nelson thought that it was perfectly grand to photograph Morgan, myself and Choux drinking coffee. To me, it seemed uneventful. We were just a small group of friends sitting around the kitchen table, getting ready to go out that evening.

Nelson's camera soon became the mainstay of his creative activity. Instead of working at home as he had in the past, preparing an opera about the astronomer, Galileo, he suddenly began attending events outside of his townhouse and would call me up to tell me about the scenes he had photographed. Sometimes, I would go out with him to different places of interest and help him with the equipment by holding his camera bag. He was fond of photographing events at *The Limelight*, a former church on 20th Street and Avenue of Americas, *The Palladium* on East 14th Street, *Danceteria* in the garment district, and the *Pyramid Club* in the East Village.

He also increased his expenditures by making duplicate copies of his tapes and hiring cars to transport him quickly to popular night spots, where the cost of admission and refreshments were always over-priced.

Chapter 2

As Nelson's relationship with Sylvia Miles intensified, he began to hire limousines to squire them around town. Sylvia had become quite popular after her appearances in *Midnight Cowboy* and subsequent films, and was invited regularly to social events in New York. As Nelson described it, the tray on a table in her apartment was always overflowing with invitations, and she would select the ones that appealed to her most. They made a smart appearance, stepping out of a limousine together, Nelson wielding his video camera, and Sylvia posing for still photographers.

One evening, he and Sylvia attended an event at the Chelsea Hotel, which featured the playwright, Arthur Miller. Nelson came back very excited about having met the renowned dramatist. Sometimes, Michael Musto would accompany Nelson on these excursions with Sylvia, but this was primarily before Michael stepped in for the *Village Voice* entertainment columnist, Arthur Bell. At the time, Michael was performing in his own band of musicians, called *The Must*, and one afternoon we went to see them play in a nightclub near Times Square. I was not particularly crazy about loud, rock and roll music, but Michael's band was well worth going to hear. Michael had an easy, almost effortless way of performing and the audience seemed to delight in his music. I would learn later, from his writing, that Michael's knowledge of popular culture extended into many fields. He'd been a journalism student at Columbia University and quickly learned to master his craft. He seemed to know everything about the world of entertainment and could discuss the work of other artists with tremendous wit, succinctly summing up the content of a new movie or play in very few words. "People used to put him down, when he was starting out," Nelson would often say. "But I told him that I thought he was brilliant and that the rest of them were wrong."

One year, Michael invited Nelson to his parents' home in Brooklyn for dinner during the Christmas holidays. Nelson was touched by this gesture of kindness and remained loyal to Michael for many years afterward. It was at one of Nelson's parties in his townhouse on Ninth Avenue, where I was able to speak to Michael for the first time. Despite his clever mind, which always seemed to be one step ahead of the conversation, Michael was remarkably sweet-natured and even somewhat shy.

When it came time for me to meet Sylvia Miles, Nelson invited me to a gathering in Chelsea (I've forgotten what the occasion was) and I mentioned to her that I'd seen a play at the New School for Social Research, similar to William Hanley's *Mrs. Dally Has a Lover*. There was a memorable line in the play, when the aging heroine, following a colloquial remark from her lover, tells the young man, "You leftover hippies are *so* articulate." This elicited a huge laugh from the audience.

"I'm a professional," Sylvia snapped. "Why would I be interested in some obscure play by an unknown writer?" Nelson, cringed. It seemed that our meeting wasn't so well intentioned, after all. But I had thought of Sylvia in watching this very original, two-character play. The part seemed perfectly suited to her and its wistful dialogue had tremendous delicacy. Instead, she would perform with Joe Dallesandro in Andy Warhol's film, *Heat*.

This first meeting did not deter me. I began writing a play for Sylvia, based on my experiences while working in the antique wholesale district of New York, at Lutfy's Antique Shop on East 11ᵗʰ Street. The play, called *Out of Antiquity*, was about a spinster saleswoman who becomes briefly infatuated with a young assistant, until the shop boy finally leaves one day. I presented it to Nelson, but he was reluctant to share it with Sylvia. "Not after your first meeting," he warned. "She's got a volatile temper, and I wouldn't want to upset her. I've seen her take umbrage with people many times." As with all of my plays that were written for famous actresses, I tried to bestow upon them a sense of dignity and depth of character that was not always apparent in the various roles they had played.

Instead, I created a portrait of Sylvia, based on a newspaper photograph of her with Pat Lawford at a social gathering in New York. "This is the *dream* Sylvia!" Nelson exclaimed. "She looks incredible!" Nelson transferred my original portrait to Ms. Miles, who confided to me later at a bar and video lounge, called King Tut's Wah-Wah Hut, "I *liked* it. But you made my eyes the wrong color."

"Oh, I'm sorry, Sylvia," I replied. "I thought that they were blue."

"They're quite obviously brown," Sylvia taunted, leaning toward my face. "Perhaps, if you ever bothered looking into them, you might see," she continued.

"How could I not have noticed?" I asked, embarrassedly.

"And you made Pat Lawford look so dike-ish!" she complained. "Anyway, I brought it to my home in Woodstock."

13

"And hid it behind the woodpile," I thought silently to myself.

Poor Pat Lawford. I had never met her and in the newspaper photo she had been wearing a woven, Chanel-styled ladies' suit. I don't know why she appeared to be masculine-looking to Sylvia in my portrait. I thought that she looked fine. "Beauty is in the eye of the beholder," as my mother used to say. I also would've liked to have heard Mrs. Lawford's opinion on the subject, but the artwork has since vanished. Perhaps my original portrait of Sylvia Miles and Pat Lawford will turn up in someone's attic, one day.

Sylvia could be fun at parties. She could also be quite terrifying to those who hovered around her. At one of Nelson's parties in his living room an acquaintance of his asked, "Do you mind if I take your picture?"

"Not, now," Sylvia replied, seated on Nelson's sofa. "I'm with my friends."

"Just one?" the young photographer asked.

"How rude can you *be*, man?" Sylvia retorted. "If you wanted to take the stupid picture, you should have just snapped it a moment ago, and not even bothered to ask."

But Sylvia seemed to forget that she was often the center of attention by the unusual choice of clothing and accessories she would wear. I thought that she looked great, when she would dress down, keeping it simple. For one of the last parties I attended at Nelson's house, she came wearing a black dress gathered at the waist, with her shoulders bare, in black hose and slippers with a black choker wrapped around her neck.

"You look wonderful," I remarked.

"Thank you," she replied, faintly smiling. By keeping it simple there had been nothing to distract one's attention from her pretty face and the lovely shape of her mature, almost matronly figure. She was a knockout in basic black.

Speaking of knockouts, Nelson was a distant relative of the famed pugilist, John L. Sullivan, although he rarely spoke about it. It was only after I asked him, one afternoon, that he shared this interesting piece of

7. Sylvia Miles at a party for the Jackie Curtis biopic, *Superstar in a Housedress*

14

information. Although Nelson was far too cultured and refined to have followed in the footsteps of John L. Sullivan, his older brother, Mark, was perhaps more physically and mentally adept for the role of a professional boxer.

Mark (or, "Marco," as Nelson called him) was a tall, good-looking lawyer, who Nelson had persuaded to move from South Carolina to New York City for the purpose of providing moral support and keeping him in familiar company. Mark had a girlfriend and seemed to enjoy living on the upper east side of Manhattan, but was also fond of taking daytrips to Atlantic City, New Jersey, where he could gamble and be entertained.

One afternoon, Nelson decided to host a party in his living room and garden. Among the guests were new tenants from the building next door, where the bodies of its former occupants had been found by New York City police officers in an apparent murder/suicide. Strangely, after the grisly discovery had been made, an examination of an interior closet revealed the bodies of two domesticated cats, who were also locked in the same deadly embrace. "Please don't say anything about it to my new neighbors," Nelson carefully cautioned Mark, Morgan Moffatt, Jamie Gallagher and me before the other guests arrived. "I wouldn't want to frighten them."

Once the invited group of Nelson's friends had assembled, and the new tenants approached the refreshment table, Nelson's brother, Mark, absent-mindedly turned to them and said, "That must have been pretty scary to hear that the police found two dead bodies in your apartment." Nelson was not within earshot of this unfortunate slip, but the new tenants were noticeably shaken.

8. *Nelson meets Jamie Gallagher*

"He tried to pick up my brother!" Nelson exclaimed about Jamie Gallagher, weeks after the evening was over. "And I'm not inviting him to anymore of my parties, so please don't bring him along." I had no idea of what had occurred between Jamie and Mark, but apparently Nelson's brother was not terribly flattered by Jamie's condolences over his verbal faux pas.

15

It was around this time that Nelson began presenting private screenings in his living room of the video tapes he had made the night before. He would often be so excited in photographing the events he attended, that he would dart with his camera from one subject to the next. "Nelson, I'm getting whiplash, just trying to keep up with the action," I complained. "The idea is to get a steady, stable shot."

"Yes, but there's always so much going on in every part of the room," Nelson would answer. "And I wanted to capture it all."

"But you haven't focused long enough on any particular subject to see and hear what they're actually saying," I continued.

"But it's *my* point of view," Nelson defended. "*I* know what they're saying."

"Very well," I sighed. "But your images are hard to follow. They're jumping all over the place."

Poor Nelson's feelings were hurt, although he understood what I was talking about and began to calm down when approaching people with his camera, eventually buying one with a built-in gyroscope to stabilize his shots. Ambient lighting in the darkened nightclubs was also a problem, and he began using a light attached to the camera to better illuminate his subjects. He also started to make audio tape recordings of every telephone call that he placed or received, which put me sometimes ill at ease. He accomplished this by attaching a suction-cupped microphone to his telephone receiver and pressing "record" on a linked audio cassette recorder.

"Why would you want a recording of every phone call?" I asked.

"To document what's been going on in my life from day to day," he answered. It made no sense to me, especially when people on the other end of his telephone line were not always aware of the recording. But apparently, he thought that his personal phone calls would someday be of interest to others.

At one point, he befriended Alexis Del Lago and began dashing around town with her, but soon realized that there were other personalities who were equally as exciting and perhaps a little less demanding. One of his favorites was Diane Brill. Diane could often be seen at *Danceteria*, looking statuesque with her spectacular figure and form-fitting gowns. I often wondered what particular talent his subjects displayed. Were they serious actors, musicians, writers, artists and dancers, or simply known for causing a sensation by their appearances in the nightclubs? We would sometime get into lengthy debates about whether it was worth all of the time and energy that he expended in following the underground scene of New York. It seemed to me that Andy Warhol had already covered this venue a decade or two earlier. But Nelson was very determined to build a reputation for himself as a chronicler of the times, no matter what the cost might be.

9. *Nelson ponders his next move at Scrabble (and the game of life)*

Chapter 3

Nelson enjoyed telling me about his life in South Carolina and his family history there. He had an Aunt, named Nancy, who had been quite lovely in youth, but was wildly free and uninhibited. According to Nelson, when his maternal grandmother had been unable to control Nancy's often rebellious, carefree nature, she subjected her daughter to a surgical procedure, known as prefrontal lobotomy. "Nancy was never the same after that," Nelson complained, "And was dependent on the family's wealth just to live."

But Nancy was his favorite relative, apart from his sibling and parents, and he loved her honest observations and freedom to roam wherever she pleased in her family-funded automobile. Nancy had allowed herself to become overweight in middle age, and Nelson was greatly amused by a colony of ants that had taken residence in his favorite aunt's car. "The thing was crawling with ants!" he exclaimed, after returning from a trip to South Carolina. "She eats constantly in the driver's seat, dropping crumbs everywhere and the ants have figured it out."

His family had made its fortune in textiles and by mining silver, but as a twelve-year-old child, he and a friend were playing among the mines when Nelson fell into a deep open shaft and had to be rescued. He'd badly injured one of his legs during the fall, and for a time his doctors were concerned that it would require amputation. His mother was greatly distressed by this diagnosis and hired specialists to save his leg. Eventually he recovered, suffering the effects of his injury in years to come. His leg would swell near the ankle when he had been overly-active, and cause him constant discomfort. He was often on his feet all day long and between his daily stint at Patelson's Music Store and his adventures at night, he would sometimes strain his injured limb beyond its endurance.

When Nelson's grandmother's health began to fail and she was hospitalized briefly, Nancy candidly remarked, "I hope that she *never* comes back," to the astonishment of other family members. But Nelson sympathized with Nancy, comparing what his grandmother had done to the efforts of Violet Venable in Tennessee Williams' screenplay, *Suddenly Last Sumer*, seeking to have her daughter-in-law lobotomized, mainly because, "She babbles."

"That horrible old witch!" Nelson would rave. "She ruined Nancy's life just to keep her subdued and prevent her from telling the truth. But it didn't work very well. Now, Nancy says whatever comes to mind and there's no way to hold her accountable."

Nelson was a kind, non-discriminating individual. It was therefore no wonder that he ventured northward from South Carolina to find freedom of expression for his creative pursuits and personal lifestyle that would not have been tolerated in his hometown of Kershaw. When the hot, humid days of summer were upon him, Nelson would stealthily climb a ladder to the community water tower, throw off his clothes and swim in its tank for relief. But his sense of abandonment did not stop there. He confided to me that as a youngster he had become romantically involved with a house servant. This was extremely taboo in his small, southern town, and reason for him to long for another life that was distinctly different from the environment in which he was raised. He was not hypocritical, but acutely aware of his own identity.

Because we were neighbors in New York, he would occasionally stop by my apartment to visit and would bring other people along. This was how Alexis Del Lago first entered my domicile, although we didn't really like each other very much. More accurately, I should say that Alexis was not terribly fond of me. But Nelson was intent that she should see a portrait I'd completed of her and James Minette, a retired female impersonator, who frequently attended plays on off-off Broadway and was closely allied with the celebrated dramatist, Charles Ludlam.

He also brought his brother, Mark, to my apartment one evening, seeking his approval by asking, "Isn't this a cute, little place?"

"Uh-huh," Mark answered with a wry smile and a nod of his head. Nelson's brother was accustomed to entering much finer digs than my own, but out of politeness, gave his tacit approval of my three-room, tenement flat.

One year, when I was especially hard pressed to pay my rent, I presented a one-act play about the flight of Jacqueline Kennedy from Texas aboard Air Force One, following the assassination of her late husband, President John F. Kennedy.

Nelson came to see the play, while Bill Miller, a reluctant participant, operated my reel-to-reel video recorder and camera to capture the unfolding drama. Elmer Kline was kind enough to introduce the performance and Nelson served as an attentive member of a noticeably sparse audience.

10. *Chris Kapp performs before Nelson as Ladybird Johnson*

Years later, I thought that Nelson had videotaped the play, himself, but this event may have occurred shortly before he acquired his first video camera. It wasn't until 2014, when I realized that a video tape of the show was among my own-reel-to-reel recordings (along with several lost tapes of Marsha P. Johnson).

Sunday, May 1, 1983
8:00 p.m.
The Survival of Jacqueline Kennedy
by Gary LeGault
starring "Ga-Ga" as Jackie
with Chris Kapp as Ladybird
RECEPTION
immediately following
pay what you wish
(suggested contribution $5.⁰⁰)
at
Ga-Ga's Funhouse 325 W. 21ˢᵗ Str.

11. *Flyer from The Survival of Jacqueline Kennedy*

Nelson was especially generous in contributing to my theatrical "rent party," leaving twenty dollars, which was only fraction of my monthly payment, but at the time, none of the other guests had any money. This was characteristic of Nelson. He was generous to a fault, advising his friends to "always tip generously." His private funds were not unlimited, however. His mother made certain that he held onto a job, even if only part-time, before sending him his monthly allowance. He had grown up with very solid, old-fashioned values. His mind was ingrained with the importance of working and being largely self-supportive. He did not display the slightest hint of being from a privileged background. He had humility, compassion, fine manners and enormous respect for other people.

The play about Jacqueline Kennedy had originally been the third part of a trilogy, entitled *Three Tragic Queens of the 1960's*. The first of the three one-act plays concerned the last evening on earth of Judy Garland and the second play depicted the final night of Marilyn Monroe. The Marilyn play was expanded into a full-length movie, shot in Hollywood several years later, entitled *The Private Life of Marilyn Monroe*. I never released it, because there were copyright issues in some of the scenes, but I sent a VHS copy of the film to Nelson and managed to earn his praise. At least, one scene from the film still exists on my Dramamonster YouTube Channel, and features Carlissa Hayden as Marilyn Monroe with Dorothy Blass (who had been Marilyn's personal secretary) as Paula Strasberg. I was proud of the work, and I hoped that Nelson would recognize how difficult it is to write, direct and produce a serious motion picture.

12. *Scenes from The Private Life of Marilyn Monroe with Carlissa Hayden and Dorothy Blass (1985)*

Nelson had taken a turn at feature film making, himself, when he was called upon to videotape a humorous satire, entitled *Mama Said*. The plot concerned a family and its cross-dressing children, with a large cast and musical numbers set in various locations around New York. He spent many months working with its creators and finally, when it was finished, he invited his friends to view the result of his labor. He was good-natured about working with the actors, although in this instance he may have benefitted from the services of a lighting designer.

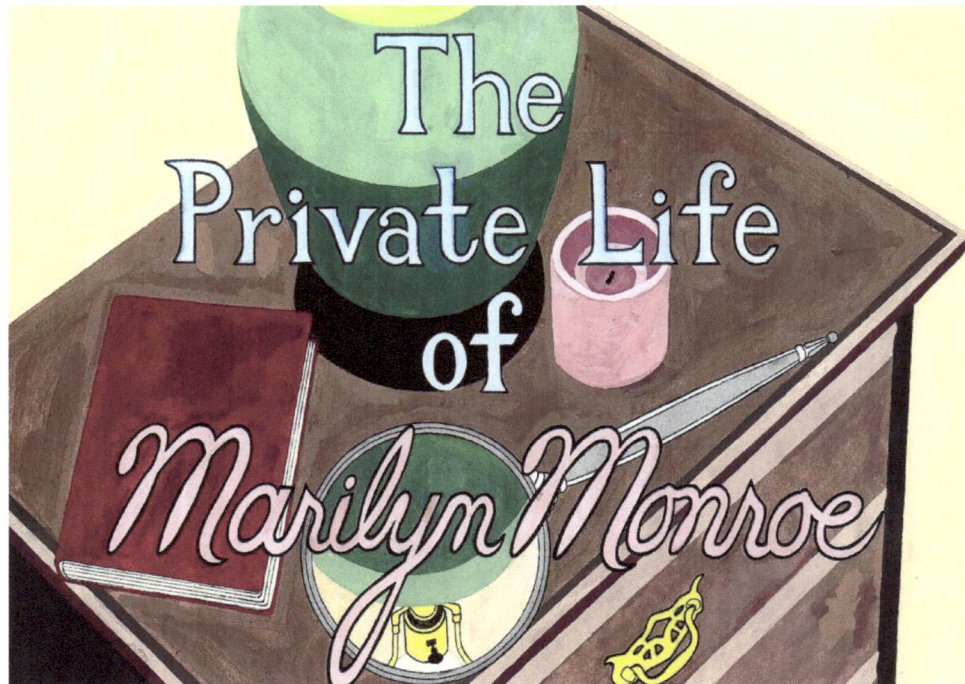

13. *Title card from The Private Life of Marilyn Monroe*

Movies were important to us. Sometime after Mae West's final film, *Sexet*, was released, Nelson and I went to see a performance at a movie theater in Greenwich Village. We aped and ogled over Mae's appearance on the screen, stunned by her bravery in trying to keep her youthful image alive, while at the same time horrified by the ravages that time had taken. We were giddy with laughter by the time we left the theater, yet fully entertained. Nelson had a mischievous quality and enjoyed witnessing performances that were slightly "over the top."

One of his favorite books, was the novel by Patrick Dennis, entitled *Little Me*. "You've never *read* it?" he asked. "Oh, but it's wonderful. It's all about the exploits an ambitious actress, named Belle Poitrine, which means 'beautiful breasts' in French!" I had seen the cover on a paperback carousel in a drugstore as a teenager, but was afraid to be caught reading it by my parents. Finally, I purchased a copy, and we would read passages from it aloud to one another. He especially loved the opening chapter, wherein Belle leaves her small, mid-western town in search of greater freedom, dismissing the townspeople as a bunch of "narrow minded, little bigots." He roared with laughter at the scene where Belle witnesses a group of disreputable

Hollywood characters sail away in an exploding showboat as she watches from the dock. For several weeks, he staggered around his living room reading aloud from *Little Me* and giggling uncontrollably. In this regard, we were alike. We both enjoyed a witty satire.

There were many walks that we took together along the Hudson River with his dog, Blackout. Nelson would always step briskly ahead of me with his dog leading the way. He adored his pets and made as much time for them as his busy schedule would allow. But at times, he seemed more than merely excited about the adventures that life in New York held for him; in truth he appeared to be quite driven by them.

One day a young man, named Jörg, arrived from Germany and landed on Morgan Moffatt's doorstep. Morgan had met Jörg at the Queen's Park in Amsterdam, several years earlier, and had kept in touch by exchanging postcards through the mail, until suddenly Jörg appeared in America with little money and in need of a place to stay. Morgan hosted him in his studio apartment for several weeks, until Jörg took up company with a young lady from Pennsylvania, who bestowed upon him a red Buick convertible. Jörg drove us on several excursions around New York and to the Palisades of New Jersey. On one of these motorized tours, Nelson, Morgan, Rhonda Granger and her boyfriend, Brant, rode along. Nelson photographed our entire time in the open car, with Morgan's hair blowing in the wind until suddenly Jörg ran past a stop sign near East End Avenue. "Jörg, you were supposed to have stopped back there," I reminded him.

"Do *you* have a driver's license?" Jörg demanded, slowing down ever so slightly.

"Well, yes, as a matter of fact I *do*," I replied. This news didn't sit too well with Jörg, who seemed indignant that a passenger in his vehicle would criticize his driving. Somehow, we made it safely back to Nelson's house and the next evening were invited to watch the video tape. It provided a good laugh for us all, but eventually Jörg married the young woman from Pennsylvania and together they drove to Florida. Jörg was tall and good-looking and had come to the United States with only the clothes on his back and his feet protected by a pair of peculiarly shaped, pointed-toed shoes. Morgan was happy to learn that Jörg walked down the aisle in the same shoes that he had arrived in, but they also added extra weight when he stepped onto the gas pedal and sped away, never to be seen by any of us again, except in Nelson's video.

Nelson would often make a duplicate tape for the subject of his videos and deliver them to the artist personally. I posted one of his earliest tapes from my 34th birthday party on YouTube, integrating my own footage of Jackie Curtis from 1978. I don't think that Nelson would have minded. He had wanted to videotape Jackie (reluctantly, at first), but missed the chance. It has racked up more views than any of my tapes of former Warhol stars or Marsha P. Johnson. Nelson also videotaped my farewell party when I left New York in 1986.

Chapter 4

One afternoon in the spring of 1984, Nelson came over to my apartment in Chelsea and was annoyed about having shared a cab with Jackie Curtis on their way home from an event on the upper east side. "I'm sick and tired of these great stars who plead poverty, when it comes time to pay their own fare!" Nelson ranted. "I was out with Jackie Curtis last night, who hitched a ride downtown in my cab, but when we got to his house, he reached into his pockets and held up two open palms with an apologetic shrug," he complained. "Imagine, the great Jackie Curtis without even enough money to chip in for a taxi!"

"But, Nelson," I defended, "Jackie doesn't have any money. He's perpetually broke. I know that it doesn't seem possible, but he struggles constantly."

"I don't care," Nelson continued. "It's ridiculous. People expect me to pay for everything, and I'm tired of it. I also work for a living."

"Jackie used to tend bar at his grandmother's saloon, Slugger Ann's Tavern, but there was never anybody in the place," I explained. "Now, that she's dead, he receives a monthly allowance, but when it's gone, he has to barter for more."

Slugger Ann's estate had been entrusted to Jackie's Aunt Josephine, who would dole out his inheritance sparingly. Often broke before month's end, Jackie would call upon his aunt to beg for more money. "I *lie* and she *screams*," Jackie would say, even though his Aunt Josephine loved him very much.

"I don't believe it," Nelson snapped.

"It's true," I explained.

"Well, I'm not falling for it, again," Nelson continued. "Who does he think he is?"

"He's a great artist," I insisted. "Haven't you ever seen one of his plays?"

"No, and I'm not going to," Nelson grumbled. Nelson looked tired. His career as a videographer had intensified and he was beginning to feel the strain.

Along about December, Jackie telephoned, and announced, "I'm rehearsing tonight, at the La Mama Annex on Great Jones Street. Why don't you come and watch us work? You might want to bring your camera, but if not, come anyway."

"May I bring a someone along?" I asked.

"Sure," Jackie said. "Just be there at eight o'clock."

Nelson and I had a habit of speaking to each other by telephone every night after we got home from work. By that time, I was sorting letters and advertisements at a bulk mail distribution company, called Mass Mailings, in Chelsea. I called Nelson around 6:00 p.m. and we began our usual conversation consisting of, "What did you do, last night?" and "What's going on, this evening?"

"Jackie Curtis invited me to sit in on rehearsal for his new play, *Champagne.*" I informed him.

"What's that about?" Nelson asked, nonchalantly.

"It's based on the movie, *All About Eve,*" I told him.

"Oh, really?" Nelson replied. "Well, that's interesting."

"He said that I could bring a guest," I continued. "Why don't you come?"

"Well, I haven't made any plans," he answered. "Oh, I suppose so, but I'm *not* bringing my camera tonight."

"And I don't feel like carrying mine," I responded. "It's too heavy. Why don't we just walk to Great Jones Street? I'll stop by your house and we can go from there."

"All right," Nelson concluded, ending our phone call.

When I arrived, however, it was snowing and Nelson paid for a cab to the east side. A rehearsal for one of Jackie's shows was often more exciting than the play's performance. His creative process was constantly evolving. When we arrived at the loft on Great Jones Street, Jackie was in his rehearsal costume, wearing a tightly fitting, lime green cardigan sweater and a flaming red wig.

One could feel the anticipation of his performance as Margo Channing, merely by stepping through the door. In the part of Eve Harrington, Jackie had cast his assistant, Mona Robson, who appeared in a shiny, yellow raincoat and hat, shivering in an imaginary alley outside of Margo's dressing room. I introduced Nelson as my guest to Jackie, who looked at him apologetically, saying, "Oh, yes. I'm glad you could come. Sit down and enjoy the rehearsal."

14. *Jackie Curtis on stage*

15. *Mona Robson*

The opening scenes of the play began to unfold with a comic pace that was so intricate and precise, we were immediately caught up in the spirit of each actor's performance. They seemed to be flying through their scenes, until the director would yell, "Cut! Now take that again." Jackie would stop, put his arm around Mona to give her encouragement, and start over. It was exhilarating to watch.

Nelson was enraptured. At one point, he turned to me and sighed. "Oh, I *wish* that I had brought my camera!"

"I know," I said. "Me, too."

But secretly, I was glad that we had left our video cameras behind. Nelson was experiencing the rehearsal through his own eyes, instead of hunched over a viewfinder. The images of Jackie would be seared into his memory, where he could replay them in his mind. I was beginning to grow weary of going out with him and the camera. It seemed to be distracting, keeping him from being in the moment of each new event, almost as though he were living vicariously through the camera and not allowing the himself to feel the thing that was happening before him. He laughed, he drew his breath and clutched my hand.

"That was wonderful! Oh, you were right," he exclaimed, as we walked back toward Ninth Avenue. "If *only* I had brought my camera!"

"Yes, but you saw Jackie in one of his plays," I said.

I hopped a plane to California for Christmas that year, and missed the play's public performance. Five months later, we learned that Jackie had died. Nelson was saddened to hear this news and so was I. Jackie had performed one of my plays, *The Roadsinger*, in a reading at the Dramatists Guild only a year before (along with Dana Higgins from *Mama Said*). He was wonderful in the part of a broken down, country and western singer. I've posted an audio recording from that night as a radio play on YouTube, but in today's world people have short attention spans and it hasn't really gotten the attention that it deserves.

Jackie gave a tender and touching performance in *The Roadsinger*, far different from his other portrayals. It also featured Jamie Gallagher as Jackie's talent manager, even though he'd been banished from Nelson's parties. Nelson attended the reading (as well as Gary Kanter), though he'd yet to see one of Jackie's signature roles.

16. *Jackie works the room*

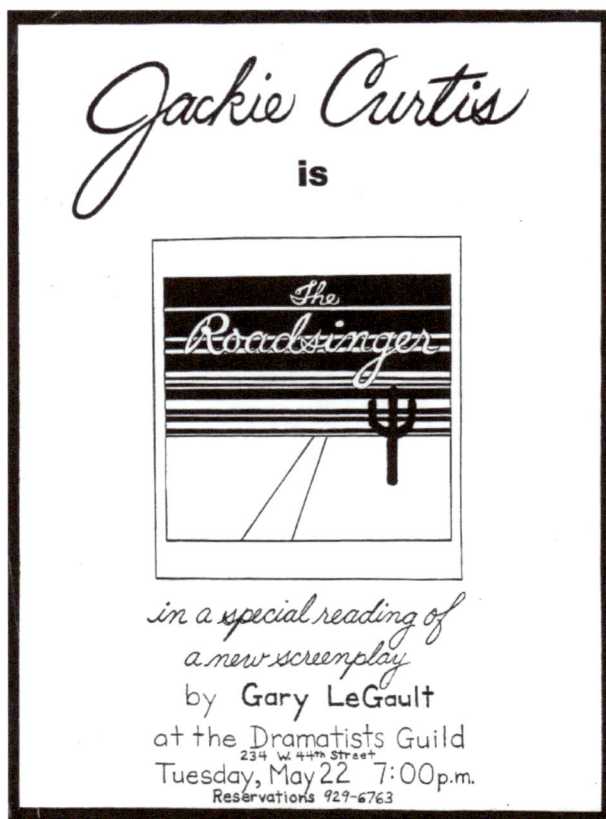

Jackie Curtis is

The Roadsinger

in a special reading of a new screenplay by **Gary LeGault** at the Dramatists Guild 234 W. 44th Street Tuesday, May 22 7:00 p.m. Reservations 929-6763

17. *Flyer from The Roadsinger reading*

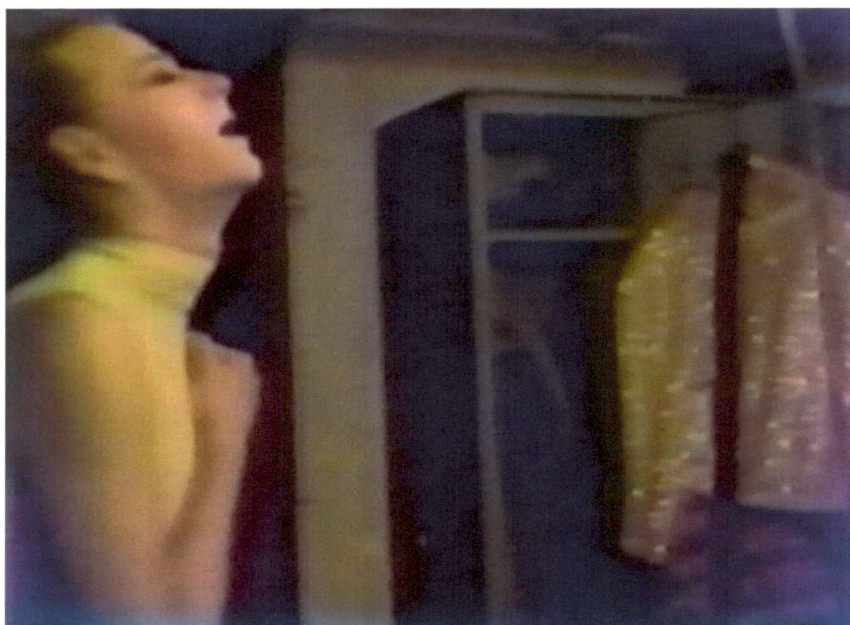

18. *Jackie in his dressing room*

Chapter 5

When my 34th birthday arrived in July of 1984, I invited a dozen guests for a party, although some of them didn't appear, making our little group all the more intimate. To my surprise (and slight consternation) Nelson showed up with his newly acquired, single unit Panasonic camera. But shortly before the guests were to arrive, I received a phone call from Rudi Berkhout, a Dutch holographer who had appeared playing a trumpet in my film, *Ina and Bruno,* and had recently set up a studio down the street in the basement of an old apartment building.

"I'm calling to invite you to my new studio," Rudi announced, after I picked up the phone.

"Well, that would be fine," I said. "But I'm having a few people over this afternoon. Would you mind if I brought them along?"

"No problem," Rudi replied.

So, our party included a field trip, while dinner simmered on the stove and Nelson followed us with his camera down 21st Street past Eighth Avenue to Rudi's basement in the middle of the block. Nelson used up two full hours of tape in photographing the event, and upon our return to my apartment, I had a difficult time getting him to put down the camera to stop and eat his meal. I was a little annoyed at the time, because I found the camera to be distracting, but in hindsight I am grateful that he brought it along. Years later (as previously discussed) it would be shown on my Dramamonster channel via YouTube in a pared down version, running twenty-eight minutes. In reviewing the tape, I was reminded of an episode that I'd completely forgotten, wherein Nelson explained that he'd just purchased the camera and had taken it out to photograph the *Gay Pride March* that year, when I'd run into him there, even holding his new portapak and taking pictures of him with it. Unfortunately, that was the year of the Summer Olympics in Los Angeles, and Marsha P. Johnson did not appear as usual in the parade down Fifth Avenue. Instead, she languished in a jailhouse near the railroad tracks of downtown L.A., where she'd been locked up on charges of prostitution. "I never imagined that the man driving a Mercedes along Santa Monica Boulevard would turn out to be a cop!" she remarked to Randolfe Wicker after returning to Newark International Airport in August.

19. *Marsha Johnson and Morgan Moffatt in Chelsea*

This came as another missed opportunity for Nelson. Whether he ever photographed the central figure of the Stonewall Riot and de facto leader of the free world remains a mystery to me. He certainly knew who she was. He may even have bumped into her a few times as she was passing through the door of my apartment in Chelsea after spending the night "conked out" in my bed, where she would sometimes retreat from the streets of New York. It's been so long, that I can hardly remember, but there were a number of guests who visited my apartment on their way up and down the ladder of success. This sliding scale of notoriety amuses me today. I'm the only one who remains in obscurity, except for Nelson's apparent belief that I was somehow worth photographing. Perhaps it was because of my early work in video, but he was kind enough to include me on many of his outings with the camera, and even seemed to have sought my approval for the path that he had chosen as a documentary filmmaker. There may have been other people running around New York with video cameras long before Nelson, including Jon Alpert and Craig Highberger, but none was more prolific than the Portapak Prince from South Carolina. For his vast body of work, I salute him, although I never fully approved of what he was doing (but more on that later.)

Sometime in the mid-1980's a group of transgender artists came up to New York from Atlanta. Nelson had a boyhood friend, named Dick Richards, who conducted interviews on cable television in the Georgian capital and they remained constantly in touch. I first met Ru Paul in Nelson's apartment after he'd arrived from Atlanta and Nelson allowed him to sleep on his living room couch. Ru was tall and slender, and very quiet as he tip-toed around the first floor with his hair cropped short, wearing cut-off jeans and a T-shirt, ambling barefooted over the dark wooden surface, much as Ava Garner had done playing the fictional character of Maria Vargas. Even without makeup, Ru was a sight to behold.

"Who's that?" I inquired after Ru had gone to the refrigerator and disappeared with a cup of yogurt.

"That's Ru Paul," he answered. His eyes beamed with fervent delight. "He's a performer. And next week, he's playing at the Pyramid Club. Would you like to join us?" I had recently videotaped Jackie Curtis at the same venue, although Jackie snatched the tapes, once they'd been recorded, and I never saw them again.

"Oh, Nelson. Not another outing," I moaned. "I mean, he's just another drag queen, isn't he?"

"Oh, no!" Nelson answered, reproachfully. "I think he's *fabulous*. And Ru Paul is going to be a big star someday."

"All right," I conceded. "If you say so."

This conversation demonstrated how incredibly wrong I could be. Ru Paul would go on to conquer the nightclubs of New York, leaving his predecessors in the dust. A few weeks later, Nelson played a video tape for me that Ru Paul had brought from Atlanta, based on the third sequence in a movie with Karen Black, entitled *Trilogy of Terror*. In Ru's film, he was pursued by a small, plaster statue, modeled after Gainsborough's *Blue Boy*. Ru Paul ran up a stairway, screaming as he tried to evade the evil statue of *Blue Boy*, wearing a tight skirt and form-fitting bodice with a wig of banana curls on his head. It was so ridiculous that Nelson and I found ourselves gasping for breath between our laughs. Tears streamed down Nelson's face as he giggled uncontrollably and I feared that I would fall out of my chair, so convulsed with laughter were we. Years later, after purchasing a copy of Ru Paul's CD, *Supermodel of the World*, with an introduction by La Wanda Page, I was persuaded that Nelson had been right. Nelson had an incredible nose for sniffing out new and exciting talent. And I no longer discount the creative efforts of anyone.

Nelson also came back from the clubs one night and brought with him a video tape he had made of Lady Bunny. In Nelson's video, Lady Bunny sauntered to the edge of the stage while clutching a microphone during her rendition of a popular tune, and toppled into the audience.

"Did she just fall off the stage?" I asked.

"Uh-huh," Nelson giggled as Bunny climbed back onto the raised platform, never missing a beat of her song and pulling her wig back into place. It was sheer insanity, but Nelson was completely caught up in it.

One evening in 1985, we were at Danceteria on West 21st Street, where I'd joined Nelson to assist with his videotaping and to watch the entertainment. Morgan Moffatt was with me, and we'd also gone to see Lari Shox, our friend and neighbor and lead singer of the band, *Shox Lumania*. "Would you just watch my camera bag, so that no one steals it?" Nelson asked as he scampered away into the vacuous, multi-leveled nightclub, photographing everything in sight.

Lari came parading past Morgan and me, wearing artificial antlers on top of his head with a long flowing cape, trailing behind him. He cast an aloof glance our way as he strutted toward the stairwell, but I had hoped that he might stop for a moment to greet his friends and prankishly stepped onto his train to gain his attention. Lari's cape, which had been attached by Velcro fasteners to the back of his leotard, snapped from his shoulders and fell limply to the floor. Morgan started to laugh, but quickly held his breath, realizing that I had caused Lari the embarrassment of a wardrobe malfunction. Noticing that something was missing from his costume, Lari retraced his steps, bent down to pick up his cape and exited in the direction of the stairwell to his dressing room in the basement.

"C'mon, let's go," Morgan insisted.

"But I'm waiting for Nelson," I replied. "He's running around with his camera."

"Oh, honestly," Morgan complained. "You're just standing there, holding someone's bag. I'm going downstairs to see to Lari."

After a while, Nelson returned and I explained to him that I had to leave with my friends. "It's all right," Nelson said. "I can carry my camera bag for the rest of this."

We said, "Goodnight," and I joined Morgan with Lari in the gloomy dungeon of his basement dressing room. "I don't get it!" Lari snapped. "After all the things I've done for you, you just want to embarrass me, when I'm out appearing before the public."

"But Lari," I tried to explain. "I thought you might stop for a moment to say, 'Hello.' I had no idea that your robe would detach from your costume."

"It was tacked on with Velcro!" Lari fumed, his antlers shaking.

I left Danceteria in disgrace and walked back to my apartment alone, giggling at the absurdity of it all. Years later, Janet Jackson would turn her wardrobe malfunction at the Superbowl into a headline grabbing sensation. If only Nelson had caught Lari's disrobing on videotape, his career might have taken off. Things can sometimes fall apart on stage, such as when I split the seam of my pants as Christopher Columbus, scaling a castle wall belonging to Ferdinand and Isabella of Spain, in my first play, "*Bravo Isabel!*" Performers should rely on underwear as they learn to adapt before an audience and use safety pins, when all else fails.

Chapter 6

One evening in 1985, Nelson telephoned me after work and said, "I'm going out to CBGB's tonight, and you're welcome to join me if you'd like."

"I'm a little tired, Nelson," I replied. "I think I'll stay at home."

"Then, why don't you come over and just hang out with me, before I leave?" he asked. "If you change your mind, we can still go together."

I accepted his invitation to visit with him while he prepared to leave for the nightclub, but was determined to spend the rest of my evening by myself. In those days, my telephone would ring repeatedly almost every night of the week with invitations to exciting things that I might see and hear in New York.

When I arrived at Nelson's, he was packing his camera bag, drinking coffee and smoking cigarettes as he scurried around the house. With a pair of VHS player/recorders he had been duplicating a video tape from his previous night's activity. He popped the finished copy out of his video deck and affixed a label onto it, after carefully writing a description of the tape's content with the date of the recording.

"I have to deliver this to the artist on my way out this evening," he said. "Are you sure you don't want to come with me to CBGB's? I'll pay for a cab."

"No, thank you, Nelson." I was out late last night and I think that I'd better rest."

"Me, too," he confided. "By the time I went for coffee after the nightclubs closed, it was 5:00 a.m. I had a terrible time, making it to work today."

"Have you rested, since you came home this afternoon?" I inquired.

"I tried to take a nap, but they've been jack-hammering in the street outside of my window," he complained. "I'm so tired. I've been dragging around all afternoon."

"Then, why don't you stay at home, tonight?" I asked.

"No, I can't." he answered. "I promised some folks that I would be there tonight."

"Who are these people, that are so important as to deprive you of your sleep?" I begged to know.

"A new band, that nobody's ever heard of," he said. "But I think they're great."

"Honestly, Nelson," I chided. "What is more important than your health? You look tired. Why don't you stay at home, tonight? All of these things will be going on at some other time, when you're feeling better."

"But Gary," Nelson replied. "I'm afraid that I might *miss* something."

"*Miss* something?" I scoffed. "You might be missing out on the rest of your life, if you don't stay at home and sleep when you're tired."

"No, no, no," Nelson insisted. "I promised them that I would be there. I can't go back on my word. Besides, I *like* doing this. It's my calling."

"And what about the opera you were composing?" I asked. "Has that fallen by the wayside?"

"I'm going to finish it one day," he insisted.

"Nelson," I pleaded, "Please stay home tonight. You look exhausted."

"I can't," he answered, matter-of-factly. "Now if you want to come with me, I'll be happy to take you along, but otherwise, I have a cab coming in ten minutes to take me crosstown."

"What does Choux think of all of this?" I asked.

"He's downstairs in his apartment," Nelson answered. "I haven't spoken to him since I got home from work."

"Why doesn't *he* go out with you tonight?" I inquired.

"He doesn't care about any of the nightlife in New York. He *hates* it," Nelson confided.

"Well, perhaps you should listen to him," I suggested, "Especially when you're run down and not feeling well."

'Oh, Gary," Nelson sighed. "No one understands what I'm trying to do. There needs to be a record of the explosion of creativity and talent that's currently taking place all over New York."

"There'll be an explosion, all right," I cautioned. "Only it won't be in any nightclub. Now, what is so special about all of these self-centered egomaniacs, that you can't simply stay at home and go to bed, when you've already been out every night in the course of a week just to appease them?"

"I've got to go," he announced, glancing out the window. "There's my cab." He carried the cup of coffee that he'd been sipping into the kitchen and dumped it down the sink. A moment later, he returned to crush his burning cigarette into an ashtray, zipped his camera bag Chouxt and picked up the portapak, walking toward the stairs. "C'mon," he said. "Maybe you'll come with me tomorrow. I'm going to the *Saint*."

"All right, Nelson," I conceded. "But I wish you'd listen to people, when they're trying to tell you something for your own good."

"I know," he said, walking briskly down the stairs. "My mother tells me all the time."

"Then perhaps, you should obey," I suggested.

"Not tonight," he concluded, opening the taxi door and climbing inside. "Call me tomorrow," he said. "I won't go out for coffee tonight. I'll come right home."

"Oh, yeah, sure." I replied, doubtfully.

"Bye, Gary!" Nelson called, as the cab sped away.

This scene was repeated many times, as I declined his invitations to join him for a night on the town. He was, in my opinion, wearing himself to a frazzle. He'd become jittery and nervous, obsessed with his camera to the point where his own physical needs were being ignored.

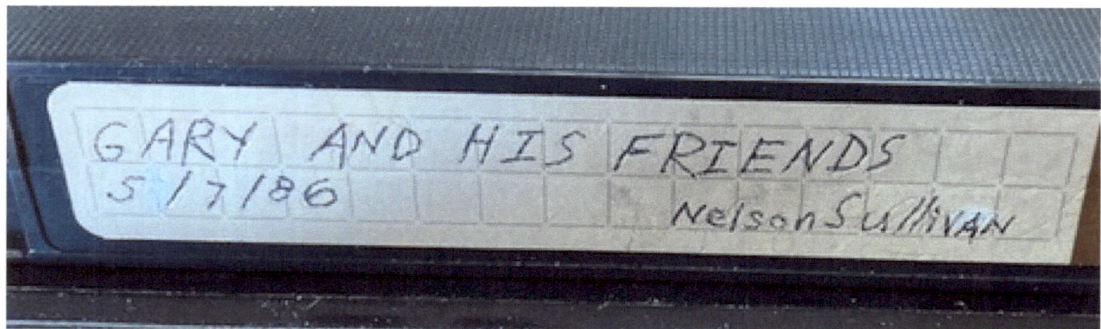

20. *A typical video tape label by Nelson*

When summer came to New York that year, I was engaged in my second season as the manager of an ice cream parlor on Eighth Avenue, called the *Chelsea Sweet Shop*. The shop was attached to a local tavern at the rear by a passage between the two storefronts. Michael Russo, its owner was nice enough to have allowed me to hang some of my original portraits in frames around the store to decorate its walls. There was an open window facing the street to serve customers passing on the sidewalk, and sometimes I would see Alexis Del Lago on her bicycle peddling along Eighth Avenue, Robert Sherman (the Mapplethorpe model), or John Reagan, who had appeared with Jackie Curtis and Holly Woodlawn in Andy Warhol's *Women in Revolt*. At least once (as I recall), during the hot summer of 1985 Nelson came into the shop to view my artworks and purchase an ice cream cone.

21. The Chelsea Twins (as seen hanging in the Chelsea Sweet Shop)

Everything was going well, until one day a young man on a bicycle came to the shop window, eating from a bunch of grapes that he held in his hands. "Can I have a bag for these grapes?" he asked.

"I'm sorry, sir, but you'll have to purchase something first," I answered.

"All right. Here's a nickel," he said, placing a coin onto the window ledge. "How about if I just *buy* a bag off of you?"

"I'm sorry, but our bags are only for customers," I replied. I strongly suspected that he had stolen the bunch of grapes from a local fruit stand in the next block along Eighth Avenue and needed to conceal his ill-gotten gain.

He hurled one of the grapes at me through the open window and cast a verbal insult, exclaiming, "Faggot!"

That did it. I walked out of the shop onto the sidewalk, tapped him on the shoulder and broke one of the basic rules of retail etiquette, "Thou shalt not *slug* the customer."

"Bam!" was the sound of my fist hitting his jaw.

"Now, you're gonna get it, asshole!" he hissed. At that point, he reached into his pocket, popped open a switchblade and stabbed me several times, before speeding away on his bicycle, ironically rounding the corner in the direction of the 10th Precinct. Fortunately, I had turned away from the deadliest insertion of his blade during our frantic struggle, and his knife slid along my ribcage, barely missing my lungs, but I was bleeding profusely from the torso. I ran back into the shop and called the tavern proprietor next door, asking for help. Within minutes, all of the barflies were out on the sidewalk, gaping at me through the open shop window as they retraced my bloody footsteps. It was complete pandemonium. Moments later a police car pulled up, and I explained what had happened as two of New York's finest officers hurried me to St. Vincent's Hospital, while I continued to bleed all over the back seat of their squad car.

It took seventeen stitches in the Emergency Room to put me back together, and afterward a patient orderly wheeled me toward a room upstairs.

"I don't want to stay here," I moaned.

"Doctor's orders," he insisted.

"But I'd rather go home," I wailed.

"Try to enjoy the hidden benefits," he assured me.

Just then, a cockroach crawled across the bed as he wheeled me into a room. "Is that one of the hidden benefits?" I asked, suspiciously.

I decided to check myself out of the hospital, which is never a good idea, but I had cockroaches of my own to nurse me at home. It was five o'clock in the morning, as I walked up Greenwich Avenue toward Chelsea, wrapped in bandages with my favorite shirt in tatters around my waist. Awash in a wave of self-pity, I stopped in front of Nelson's townhouse, and rang the bell. Moments later, Nelson's head extended from his third-floor bedroom window, as he wearily inquired, "Gary, what's wrong?"

"I was stabbed with a switchblade!" I hollered up the side of the building.

"Oh, my God!" Nelson gasped in horror. "I'll be right down."

I heard him hastily running down the wooden staircase, before throwing open his door. "What happened?" he asked.

"Oh, I slugged some guy outside of the shop, for calling me the F-word," I answered. I've been up at St. Vincent's all night, while they stitched me back together. They wanted me to stay longer, but I decided to go home."

"Can you make it the rest of the way on foot?" he asked. "Do you want me to call for a cab?"

It's only seven blocks from here," I replied. "I can walk them. But would you mind coming over later, just to see that I'm still alive?"

"Of course," he answered. "Let me go back to bed, and I'll come by after work."

By the time Nelson arrived at my apartment in Chelsea during the late afternoon, there was a lively party going on. Elmer Kline, Morgan Moffatt and Bill Miller were there, trying to cheer me up as I ran around the kitchen opening cans of beer. Elmer kept making jokes, even though it pained me to laugh. Nelson walked in with a bag full of groceries. He was all sympathy and grace and so kind to have gone shopping for me. Morgan wept tears of relief to see that I was ambulatory and agile and I learned how dear my friends really were to me. There are no better people than the friends one makes in New York. And there is no greater police force in the entire world. When my apartment had been burglarized in 1978 and my SONY monitor and new, color video camera had been stolen, a clever detective spotted the thieves boarding the Seventh Avenue subway and arrested them at gunpoint with the camera (still attached to its tripod) protruding from a plastic trash bag. This was an omen, I surmised, that I should finish creating *Ina and Bruno*. I would never had met Nelson, otherwise.

22. *Elmer and Nelson perform a skit in costumes from* Ina and Bruno

Chapter 7

A few weeks after the stabbing incident, Nelson telephoned one day to tell me that he'd rented a movie in VHS format at his local video store, and invited me to watch it with him in his living room. "What's it called?" I asked.

"*Peeping Tom*," he answered. "Have you ever *seen* it?"

"No," I replied. I'd seen *Tom Thumb* with Russ Tamblyn, as a child, but this was a tale of someone named Tom that I hadn't heard of.

"Why don't you come over and we'll watch it together?" he asked.

"Shall I bring anyone?" I inquired.

"That's all right," Nelson replied. "Just come by yourself."

"I've never heard of this film, before," I continued. "Is it any good?"

"I'll let you decide," he answered. "It was made in England, by a director named Michael Powell and released in 1960. It stars a German actor, named Carl Boehm and Moira Shearer, in case you're not familiar with the film's director."

I'd seen Moira Shearer in *The Red Shoes*, a famed British dance film that ends tragically, when a ballerina cannot remove a pair of bedeviled toe shoes that lead her onto a railway track. "How lovely," I thought. "Perhaps Moira will dance in this one."

"All right," I agreed. "I'll come watch it with you."

"See you at eight o'clock," Nelson said, happily.

When I arrived at his townhouse, Nelson was completely alone. He prepared me for the screening of the film by offering me a small glass of wine, while he sipped a cup of coffee. The film began to play and I noticed one murder, two murders, until finally, lovely Moira Shearer was slain in front of the photographer's camera during the course of the movie. What's the matter, Gary? Nelson asked with a mischievous gleam in his eye. "Don't you *like* this movie?"

"Well, I was hardly expecting it to contain so much violence," I answered.

Peeping Tom is about a photographer who slays his victims by use of a dagger concealed in the tripod of his camera. It bears psychological ramifications about voyeurism and the power of an artist over a model, or the subject of an artist's work. I was influenced as a youngster by a poem, entitled *My Last Duchess*, by Robert Browning, wherein the narrator retains a portrait of each of his past wives, who have all come to an unfortunate end. The idea of keeping a portrait of someone long after they were gone, intrigued me. But certainly, I was not into the kind of violence displayed in *Peeping Tom*, wherein each victim suddenly realizes that she is about to be murdered in front of a camera. Nelson's screening of the film for me was especially uncomfortable in light of the fact that I'd been stabbed by a knife wielding assailant only a few weeks earlier, and he seemed to take a certain degree of pleasure in watching my reaction to the death scenes. The film didn't bother me very much, however. What annoyed me was his slightly warped sense of humor by inviting me over to see it and his delight in replaying the enactment of each murder while asking, "What's wrong?"

In reviewing the long version of his video tape from my 34th birthday, I discovered a segment near the end, wherein Elmer Kline says to Nelson, "You look like so much Edgar Allan Poe."

"Thank you," Nelson responds. "Sometimes I fancy that, that I may be Edgar Allan Poe."

"You need a long, flowing tie on," Elmer continues.

"A plume. I need to have a plume in my hand at all times," Nelson remarks. Edgar Allan was my hero."

Nelson was an avid reader. It is interesting that Poe's most famous short story, *The Gold Bug*, was centered on Sullivan's Island off the coast of Charleston, South Carolina, and that Nelson would live to be slightly one year beyond Poe's age, when he died.

"My sister was named after one of his poems," Elmer went on to say in the video tape.

"Annabelle Lee?" Nelson asked.

"No, *Lenore*," Elmer replied.

"Da-da (sorrow) for the lost Lenore," Nelson followed, mistakenly quoting from *The Raven*.

"Right. My mother was very romantic, except for my name, *Elmer*."

"I call that *Gothic*," Nelson said in the video tape. This portion of the tape was shot by myself, picking up the camera to capture a little of the filmmaker as a subject, in his own production. In hindsight, Nelson's dissipation appeared to be more rapid than Poe's. From the images on video tape of Nelson that were captured by my camera in 1983 to those that appear in his own work near end of his life, one can sense a pervasive weariness that seemed to engulf him. It was as though he had stepped into of pair of red shoes when he picked up the camera and could not put it down.

I was sad to see this. We had only been friends for four years, when I left New York in 1986. But within three additional years, he would be dead.

Several days after my violent attack by a switchblade (brought on by my own unruly behavior), Nelson revisited me in Chelsea and we climbed the stairs to the roof of my apartment building, carrying a couple of bentwood chairs, upon which we sat in the sunlight, talking.

"I'm ready to leave New York," I announced.

"Gary, no!" he objected. "Everything's happening here. Think of all of the exciting events that you're invited to. What better place is there for an artist to be?"

"But it's going on fifteen years, Nelson," I lamented. "I'm getting nowhere as an artist, and I might just as well live somewhere else."

"Where?" Nelson asked.

"Well, I can always return to California. I grew up there and have family and friends who might remember me," I replied.

"But we *need* you in New York," Nelson encouraged.

"Oh, nonsense. There are plenty of others ready to take my place. They arrive by the busload. Haven't you been to the Port Authority Terminal? You'll see them there."

"Honestly, Gary," he said. "I think you're making a mistake."

"Oh, I don't think so, Nelson. There comes a time, when enough is enough. How many more bad plays on off-off Broadway do I have to witness? I've hammered on the door of every major theatrical producer in New York and tried numerous times to get an agent, but if they don't know you, they're not interested."

"Well, I think that you're very talented," he assured.

I had given him a framed portrait taken from a still segment in my video tape of our Scrabble game during 1983. It depicted a profile of his head with his wavy hair prominently featured. He had taken the colored-pencil drawing and placed it somewhere in his bedroom on the third floor of his townhouse, although I don't remember exactly where. I thought that it was pretty good, but there were other portraits he acquired over the years that have reappeared on the Internet, whereas my profile of Nelson seems to have vanished. I wondered whether Nelson's brother might have inherited it as part of the estate, but after reading about Mark's death in 2017, the riddle remains unanswered. I hope that if someone finds it one day, he (or she) will realize how carefully crafted and what a special gift it was to person it portrays

.

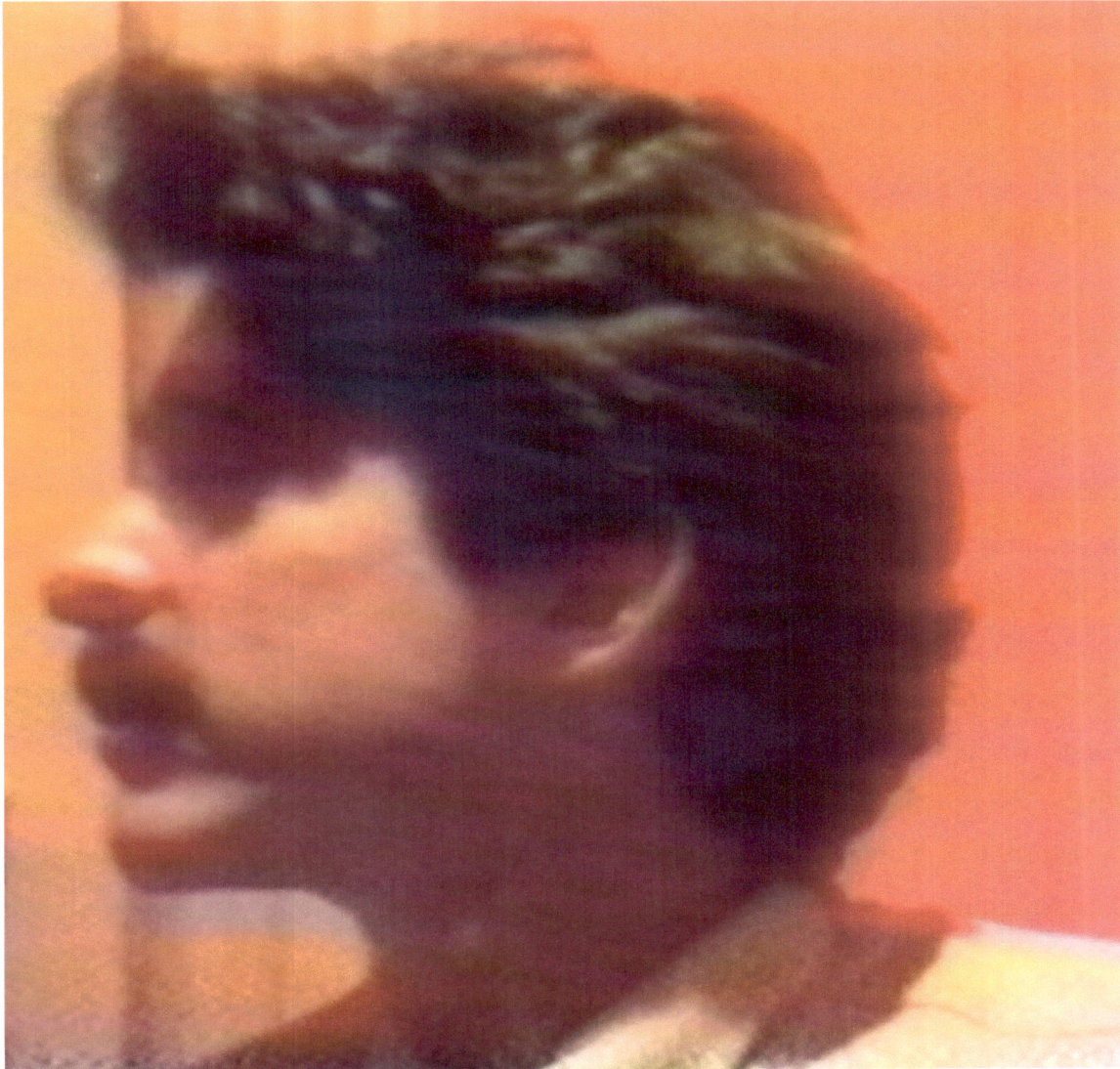

23. *Nelson in profile (1983)*

There was another of my drawings that he admired of a doorway in my block on 21st Street between Eighth and Ninth Avenue. It displayed the name, Sophia, engraved into the glass of a vestibule door to a tenement building. I was quite taken with the engraving, each time I passed, because of the enduring love it portrayed by the builder for a woman named Sophia. Jackie Curtis took the original portrait in exchange for his appearance in the reading of my play, *The Roadsinger*, at the Dramatists Guild. "Well, I might as well get something for doing this," he declared. "May I have the portrait of that doorway? I mean, the name, *Sophia*, that's got to mean something to someone."

"Of course, you may have it, Jackie," I said, taking it down from the wall where it had been hanging. I was reluctant to give it away. It was a special favorite of mine, but it was very hard to say, "No," to Jackie, especially when he was performing in my play for gratis. Only a color slide of the original portrait remains in my possession, courtesy of my actor/photographer friend, Dan Strickler. Perhaps the original drawing may be found among Jackie's personal effects that were acquired by his cousin, Joseph Preston. But several years later, I attempted to recreate the portrait with less satisfactory results.

Nelson always kept his eyes open for beauty that seemed to abound everywhere and once he acquired his camera there was no stopping him from picking it all up.

25. *Doorway at 311 West 21st Street NYC 10011 (recreation of original)*

26. *Detail from doorway*

24. *Doorway at 311 West 21st Street New York City 10011*

Chapter 8

It was the beginning of the end, however. For all of our adventures together, despite the excitement of New York and my wonderful friends there, I had grown weary of life among the granite sky scrapers, rumbling subways and jostling crowds. Jackie Curtis had passed away, shortly after an opportunity arrived to present my screenplay, *The Roadsinger*, as a motion picture in Hollywood. In retrospect, it would've been better to have persuaded Jackie to join me in the western film capital, but I failed to mention him in the deal that I'd been making before his death interceded. Consumed with vanity, I stepped into the role of Billy Brody, myself, and was downright awful in the part. "He never *did* learn," Jackie would say. "That's what they should put on your tombstone."

I bristle when people claim to have "no regrets," after enjoying a long and meaningful life. I have an ample list, a "trail of tears," as the native Americans have been known to say. But nowadays, the northern tribes have their own gambling casinos, convincing me that there *is* universal justice, after all.

I had a chance meeting with Gary Kanter, before leaving New York. One afternoon, I persuaded Morgan Moffatt and Jamie Gallagher to come with me to the newly created, *Museum of Broadcasting*, on Manhattan's upper east side. We had just finished watching Mary Martin as *Peter Pan* (a role that Jackie Curtis had longed to play), when the museum's docent hauled out a VHS copy of the Lucy and Desi Comedy Hour, guest-starring Tallulah Bankhead. It was quite a double feature, but a short distance away I heard someone laughing in another video booth, and recognized the voice as Gary Kanter's. He came over to join us while watching Tallulah fool around with Lucy and we laughed so heartily that the docent returned to ask whether we might pipe down. But Gary (like Nelson) has a flawless eye and ear for talent, and since my departure from New York, I rely on him to keep me apprised of the best new theatrical entertainment America has to offer.

I wasn't quite finished in Manhattan, however (nor was New York yet finished with *me*). As soon as my ill-conceived, video production of *The Roadsinger* was completed in Los Angeles, I boarded a plane to Kennedy International Airport with a copy of the movie in hand, and resumed living for a short time at my apartment in Chelsea.

45

"Why don't you present it at King Tut's Wah-Wah Hut?" Nelson asked. "You could have a public showing and we could all watch it together." To my surprise, I contacted the manager of King Tut's and he was happy to schedule a screening. Unfortunately, I was extremely nervous about playing the star-crossed country and western singer, Billy Brody, while the waiters kept coming around with pitchers of beer. By the time the movie was over, I was stewed to the gills. I can't remember whether people were laughing, or jeering at my melodramatic, videotaped performance, although I somehow managed to squeeze into a cab with Morgan, Nelson and a few others after it was over and we all headed back to Chelsea.

27. *Scenes from The Roadsinger with Frank Lee White, Laura Perdue, Dot Cannon, Ann Zeitlin and the author*

To complicate matters, upon our arrival Morgan and I wandered into a local tavern, where I met an unsavory character who'd recently been paroled from a penitentiary (although this was unknown to me at the time). Over Morgan's protests, I invited this fellow back to my apartment where he attempted rob and kill me (as would the movie critics), but I managed to subdue him, breaking the fifth metacarpal of my left hand and acquiring a pair of swollen, blackened eyes in the scuffle. Once my assailant was safely in jail, I negotiated a buy-out of my apartment lease, and prepared to leave town.

Only Elmer Kline was sad to see me go. Strangely, the others appeared to be somewhat relieved. While my wounds subsided, I took up residence in my high school friend and fellow-actor, Dan Strickler's, apartment at the Manhattan Plaza during his absence for an out-of-town engagement.

Nelson videotaped my farewell party there. I haven't posted it on YouTube, but perhaps I shall one day. I was not at my best in front of Nelson's camera, explaining my injuries by saying that "I slipped on the ice." But the month was May, and there wasn't any ice, except in Dan's refrigerator.

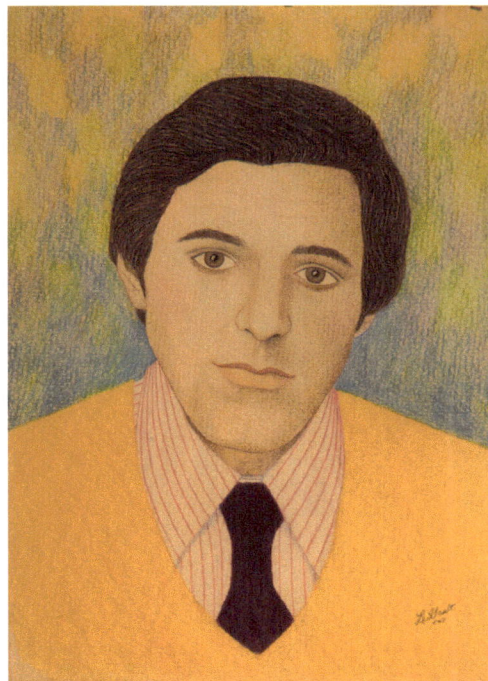

28. *Dan Strickler (1979)*

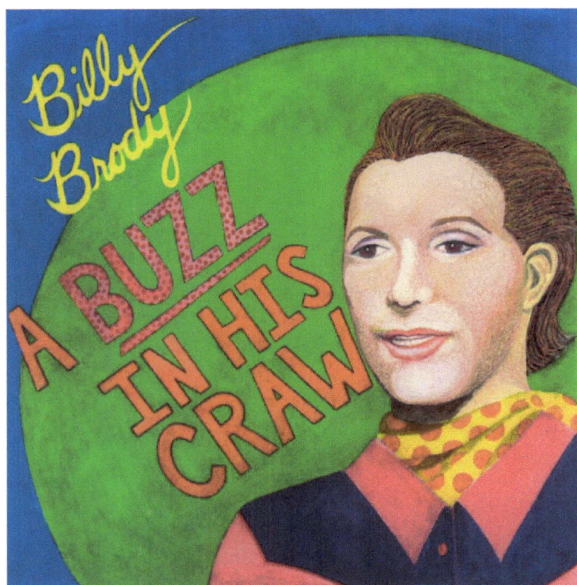

29. *Billy Brody album cover featuring Jackie Curtis*

Nelson continued to pursue his passion as a videographer, and about a year after I'd returned to California, he telephoned to tell me that he was planning a trip to San Francisco with his camera to "soak up some local color." I offered to drive to San Francisco from Los Angeles and join him while he was visiting California, but when the day of my departure came, Nelson said, "You'd better not come, Gary. I've got too much to do, and there just isn't enough time."

30. *Farewell to Chelsea - Morgan Moffatt, Jamie Gallagher, Lari Shox and the author (hiding behind dark glasses)*

That was the last time that I ever spoke to him. A year later, Morgan telephoned to tell me that Nelson had died from an apparent heart attack, although the details of his passing remained unclear. I felt terrible for Nelson, and also for his devoted dog, Blackout, who Nelson had rescued as a stray animal, wandering the streets during one of New York's great electricity failures. I remember it well. I'd eaten frozen food from a local grocery store afterward, and was stricken by food poisoning that lasted for days. I also wondered how Nelson's brother, Mark, would accept the news of his death, as well as his mother and his beloved Aunt Nancy.

Many people were charmed by him. But some of those who knew him were also alarmed by his rapidly changing behavior. He seemed to be on a relentless track that would ultimately extract a terrible price. The AIDS epidemic had been sweeping New York and Nelson described its unsuspecting carriers as "ticking, little time bombs." He often wondered aloud, "Can you imagine that something you might have done years ago, would all of a sudden, sneak up and kill you?"

I learned that Choux had moved out from the ground floor apartment of the townhouse they remodeled together and Nelson had claimed it for himself, leaving the upper floors to his guests. I felt especially sorry for Choux. He loved Nelson better than anyone. But there was nothing that he or anyone else could do. As a man of style and means, Nelson unwittingly became the architect of his own demise. Perhaps this theory is difficult for his followers to accept. But it was also quite painful for those who knew him to see his tragedy unfolding before their very eyes. He was a sweet, darling man, one who was loved by all.

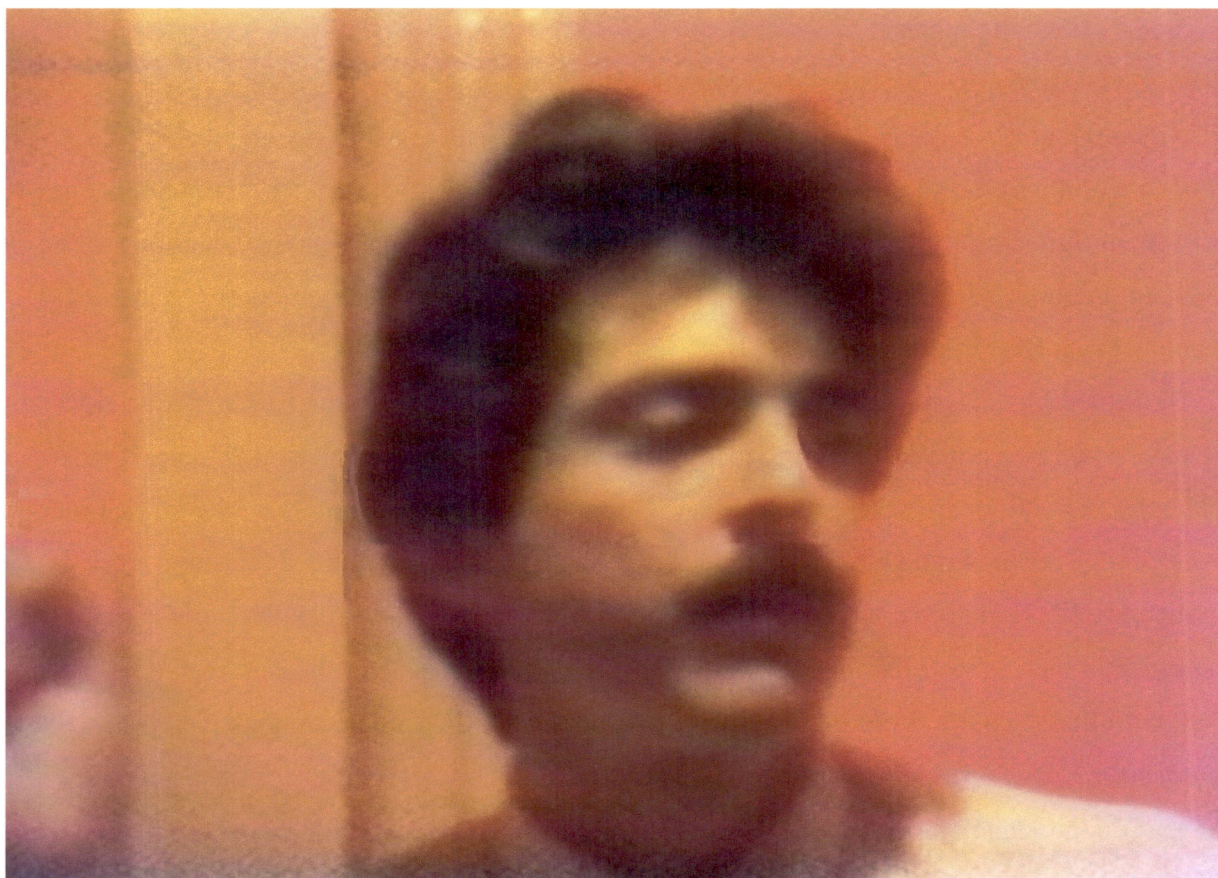

31. *Lovable, likeable Nelson Sullivan*

Chapter 9

Years later, on the last day of filming for my film, *East of the Tar Pits* in California, I attended a party with Holly Woodlawn, hosted by Adriano Serafini. I was speaking to Holly, when a young man walked up to us and asked, "Are you Gary LeGault?" Nobody ever recognizes me, so I was a bit surprised.

"This is Robert Coddington," Holly said, introducing us. "I've spoken of him before."

"I'm Nelson Sullivan's archivist, and I recognized your voice from his first video tape recording," the young man said.

"Well, yes. I *am* Gary LeGault," I answered. "How do you do?"

"I *thought* that it was you," he said. "I could tell by your voice. And I'm fine, thank you."

I have a brother who sounds just like me. People mistake us for each other on the telephone. But I was intrigued by Robert Coddington. I never fully imagined that anyone would be willing to pick up the torch where Nelson had dropped it, but there he was standing before us in Adriano's West Hollywood patio.

I *like* Robert Coddington, although I've given him lot of grief over the years with questions such as, "Could you tell me something that I don't already know about Nelson?" I hate it when people pull rank on me, but there I was doing it to poor Robert. He is, however, the embodiment of everything Nelson would have wanted his archivist to be. He has elevated Nelson's work as a documentary filmmaker to international standing. I also watched him skillfully negotiate Holly's appearance at the *Torino Film Festival* with its visiting director in 2010. Nelson would be so proud of all that Robert has done to bring his work to the public's attention. Personally, I no longer care whether others embrace my creative pursuits. The works speak for themselves. We're all on our separate paths, moving in our own direction, but occasionally, those paths intersect. And there should be no competition between artists, as far as I'm concerned.

When Holly Woodlawn was dying, and I was prohibited from seeing her at the last nursing home where she stayed in Los Angeles, her guardian telephoned and said, "Anyone who thinks that he is the next Andy Warhol, is definitely *out*."

"The *next* Andy Warhol?" I thought to myself. "Wasn't one of them, *enough?*"

Many people gathered around Warhol with the hope that his celebrity might rub off onto them. Much to his credit, Andy was accessible to almost anyone who wanted to sit and talk with him or visit his factory. I asked Bob Colacello to consider my screenplay, *Ina and Bruno*, for a possible production. Warhol declined, but was still very nice to me. That didn't mean that my work really stinks. It only smells a little. And a slight sense of humor (like humility) goes a long way, especially among those who are easily offended.

Nelson had those traits. He didn't seek to impress or compete with anyone. Like it or not, he was on a mission that he completely determined for himself. There is no crossover between his work and Andy Warhol's. Nelson was in a category and a class of his own.

And by the way, I *like* Holly's guardian. He didn't intend to dismiss me; he merely voiced his suspicion of what people are often up to and was doing his job to shield her from further distress. I'm no angel, nor was Nelson. Jackie Curtis used to say, "People don't understand me, but I'm *flesh* and *blood*." It is very difficult to succeed as an artist on *any* level. Ultimately, the success or failure of a work is determined by the artist, herself. As Paulita Sedgwick often told me, "You cannot *rush* a work of art."

32. Paulita Sedgwick on Bank Street (1978)

That's why it's taken me so long to write this book, although it doesn't really matter, anymore. I'm still alive, whereas others are not. But when it's late at my home in the desert and the wind howls outside of the door, I think of them. They visit me while I'm sound asleep. I'm back in my apartment in Chelsea. I can see and hear them all so vividly. What do people really mean to one another? Why do they come into each other's lives? Was it the plight of a youth interrupted that causes them to cast such a deep, lingering shadow? Is it the longing for a time gone by that makes them so desirable, unattainable, yet all the more real? I hear them. They whisper and amble. They sing to me softly.

33. Old B. Altman's Department Store loading dock in Chelsea (1994)

Nelson and I passed this site many times. I always pointed it out to him as a solitary place that I stumbled upon during my first week in New York. It haunts me still as I await his return in a taxi that calls but for me.

34. *The author with Tom Claypool and Gary Kanter (1984)*

Afterword

I guess I really *am* like Belle Poitrine, just as Nelson suspected. I certainly had enough blind, unbridled ambition. But somehow, he managed to subdue my desire to always be at the center of my own world and recognize that there is great talent everywhere.

Nelson particularly loved flea markets and public art shows. He never knew what he might find there: an unusual pair of shoes, an old piece of sheet music, an entertaining book or a colorful necktie.

I offered to take him to see Minette at his apartment in Brooklyn.

"Can I bring my camera?" he asked.

36. *Recovering in Capistrano*

"No, I'm afraid not," I answered, "No, I don't think so."

"Then, I don't want to go there," he decided.

Another missed opportunity, as far as I could see. Visiting Minette was like entering another world. Camera in hand or not, it was

35. *At an amusement park in New Jersey*

well worth the experience. But this is where our story ends. Nelson and I suffered from irreconcilable differences. He wanted to capture everything on video, although I more often wanted to live the experience and draw from it. Thank goodness, he never listened to me. But I miss him.

37. *Richard Chamberlain as Hamlet*

Jamie Gallagher took my portrait of
Richard Chamberlain as *Hamlet* when I was
disposing of my possessions in New York.
That would be the last I'd see ever see of it.
Nelson bought my Georgian mantlepiece
and mahogany writing desk. Minette
purchased my Victorian loveseat. The
peacock chair that Jackie filled so well and
so often disappeared on a bicycle after I had
set it out to be reclaimed upon the sidewalk.
Whooosh! And it was gone.

38. *Jackie Curtis in Chelsea*

But there was a time when all of us were together, before the increasing pace of New York
City nightlife overtook us one by one. A time for parlor games and conversation. A time to
dream of things to come. A time to share as friends.

39. *Nelson and the boys play a game of Scrabble*

40. *Marsha P. Johnson visits in the kitchen*

41. *Paulita Sedgwick and the author (in his favorite shirt)*

42. *The End*